The Secret Desserts of Life

Savor the Richness of Your Abundance

By

Reverend Carrie Carter

Acknowledgements

I would like to acknowledge my Angels and Guides especially MY Guardian Angel David who has been there and supported me as long as I can remember. I would like to acknowledge the tens of thousands of clients who had faith in me and my spiritual gifts.   I would like to personally thank Randy Gage, his Prosperity seminars and teachings that have brought me into a new awareness of Prosperity and Abundance that I have in my life! I would like to personally thank Lisa Jimenez MY Life and Success Coach extraordinaire! We have just begun to soar! Thank You to Catherine Ponder and her Book "The Dynamic Laws of Prosperity." A Very Special thanks to Dr. Caron B. Goode for without her special intuition and talents of research the writing this workbook would have been difficult to process.

Dedication

I would like to dedicate this book to my fiancée and Life Mate, Jim

Overholser., whose. faith in me and love has helped me feel free to claim

the Prosperous and Abundant Birthright which is ours for the asking

Introduction

With this course, I want to help you attract the abundance in your life which is your birthright. I will give you twenty-two days of abundant thinking and practices to help you manifest your greatest desires. I will share with you how to get rid of the blocks that keep you from your abundance. You will gain understanding of the Universal Laws of Abundance and learn how to attract all the abundance you so desire and deserve.

Each lesson is organized in this way:

1. An Angel Quote introduces the topic and inspires your abundance thought for each day.

2. The abundance lessons are provided with the help of angelic friends.

3. The exercise that follows each abundance lesson provides you with an opportunity for direct experience of the lesson by enhancing your

intuition and awareness, and teaching you to observe abundance in your world.

I designed each exercise page so you can make multiple copies. Each time you experience an abundance lesson you will learn and go deeper into your knowing of abundance. I encourage you to go through the sequence of lessons; copy enough exercise sheets so you have fresh journal material; and then repeat the entire sequence of lessons again. The consistent and positive focus on abundance is the strength of manifestation.

The The Secret Desserts of Life

By

Reverend Carrie Carter

Angel Quote 1

*Abundance is your birthright
not something you need to earn.
Start claiming it.*

Lesson 1

Abundance Is Your Birthright

Abundance is not something we acquire. It is something we tune into.

Wayne Dyer

Your lesson for today is to know one truth: Your God-given birthright is for you to be abundant in all things. Are you ready to learn how to achieve that birthright?

It is your birthright to be abundant. Everybody wants abundance in their lives; and we deserve to live our lives blessed with money, health, happiness, and great love. Abundance is your birthright because God created us in his own image, and He is abundance manifested. Life is too short to settle for anything less than full prosperity.

God's love flows through all of us simultaneously, connecting one to each other. If we become abundant and happy in our lives, we will connect to others who share the same wealth and abundance. The love and abundance that flows through each of us has the potential to affect every person.

What a phenomenal privilege to experience the richness of life in this buffet of experience. Nature's wealth surrounds us. The endless heavens reflect creation's abundance.

Imagine a vast ocean of God's love that is available at every moment. We can consciously visualize this love as ocean waves moving to us because the human bodies are vessels, containers of God's love.

Knowing that we are made in God's likeness offers us the opportunity to feel this love in our core and call upon it for manifesting our abundance.

Prosperity starts with knowing this core truth in our hearts and believing it: Every cell in our bodies is a contained universe within itself, nourished by the ocean of love. It exists within us and without.

The life force constantly replenishes our spirit, our essence. When we truly

recognize the Source within us, we are aware of our birthright.

Holding this knowledge of birthright in our consciousness every day

resonates in you and around you. What you focus on, you attract.

Exercise 1

Guided Imagery

I relax, close my eyes, and settle into a calm state of being. My mind is calm and open. My heart is calm and receptive. My body is relaxed and alert. Within my mind, I create a vast ocean that I imagine to be the immensity of God's love. The ocean is the potential of all creation, and the original force moving into my world.

I imagine that I stand tall and erect, facing the gentle waves that softly kiss my being and invite me to swim in the abundance of God's love. I walk toward the ocean and slip slowly into the warm waves. I float and feel safe in the buoyant waves. I breathe in God's love. The ocean of love seeps into my pores, and circulates through my body and brain.

I slowly sink to the depth of all potential, and transform into a dolphin. I am the different creature who lives in this depth and knows the feeling of love and safety. I am free. I feel rich. I am love. I am abundance.

Like the dolphin, I swim through God's abundant potential to imbibe and embody the fullness of this Love experience. Now I am silent and let my experience unfold.

When complete, open your eyes, breathe deeply, and allow the body to move as needed. Completely feeling embraced by the abundant energy that flows through you and the Universe making us ALL connected as one…

Angel Quote 2

You do reap what you sow.

Spread only happy thoughts throughout the universe.

Lesson 2

The Law of Compensation

Most people today still have to learn that they cannot get something for nothing, but must give before receiving or must sow before reaping. When they do not give or sow in terms of prosperity, they make no contact with God's lavish abundance; and so there is no channel formed through which the rich, unlimited substance of the universe can pour forth its riches to them.

-Catherine Ponder-

Today, take time to reflect upon the Law of Compensation, which means that what you reap is what you sow. To reap abundance in your life, first look at what you have sown. What you sow is what you give out or put into the world. What you reap is what you take back from the world or what the flow of life delivers to you.

When you give from your heart, God gives back to you. If you want to attract money into your life, then use it to make God's world a better place. Whatever you give comes back to you tenfold. If you give out positive thought and love, you will get back the same. When you put forth negative thoughts, they will return to you.

You can attract abundance by doing good things for yourself, for others, and for God's world. Feed the birds, donate time to your favorite charity, and give those dollars to the musician playing on the street. Perform random acts of kindness for others. I often pay for a stranger's dinner, and instruct the server to tell them that an angel picked up the tab.

Perform these kind actions with an open heart and without expectations of return. You will not always get the specific item back as you have given. Yet the universe brings to you a return on your investment. For instance, you might pay for a stranger's dinner; and then you get a phone call from your child who you had not heard from in years.

The reverse is also true. You could have been short-tempered with a loved one in your life before she or he went off to work, and then someone cuts you off on the expressway. This law is in effect for all of us always. None of us can avoid it.

To reap the abundant blessing you deserve in your life; think, and do only good to yourself and to others. I know you can do it.

Exercise Two

Paying Kindness Forward

For the next seven days, perform two acts of kindness anonymously, and enjoy the richness of your love going into the world through your positive actions. Keep your record on the next page:

DAY	ACT 1	ACT 2
1		
2		
3		
4		
5		
6		
7		

Angel Quote 3

*Add color to your world and
create a rainbow of abundance for yourself*

Lesson 3

Colors of Abundance

Empty pockets never held anyone back.

Only empty heads and empty hearts can do that.

Norman Vincent Peale

What are the colors that attract abundance to you? I hope from your focus on abundance principles in your life that you can feel the positive energy growing in your universe. Today, I share with you which colors to surround yourself with to attract abundance to your life.

Angels tell me that certain colors evoke spiritual power. So it is good for you to wear certain colors, to surround yourself with color vibration, and even to eat the color combinations that correspond to the type of abundance you want to attract in life.

You can use any specific color on the following list to attract certain types of abundance. Consciously set your intention to do so.

Color	Attracts to You
Green	Prosperity & easy money
Gold	Riches & wealth in business
Silver	Genuine friends
Brown	Acquire land & new homes
Purple	Spiritual awareness
Pink	Love to you from others and for yourself
Red	Energy when worn as a power color
Blue	Intuitive emotions & expression
Yellow	Intelligence increase and friendships
White	Purity of thought and spiritually connects you to your angels
Indigo	Blessings from the Angel and Spiritual Truths within ourselves

Exercise 3

Wearing Colors of Abundance

Now that you have the color list, it is time to choose what you wish to attract. Choose the clothes to wear and the foods to eat. Then, surround yourself with the colors to pull toward you the kind of abundance you seek. For this exercise, pick one color and bring it abundantly into your life for the magical number of 3 days. Wear the clothes, carry a stone in your pocket, set a candle on your desk, and eat the foods. Each day, make a few notes about what you observed:

What the universe brought me today was...............

I noticed that my thoughts are............

The colors make me feel............

The people around me ...

Spiritually, I am aware of ....

What struck me most about the power of this exercise is.................

Angel Quote 4

*Tithing ten percent of your income
brings to you a hundred percent profit*

Lesson 4

The Law of Tithing

Your prosperity consciousness is not dependent on money; your flow of money is dependent on your prosperity consciousness.
Louise Hay

The angels recommend that to be abundant and prosperous, it is good to practice the Law of Tithing. This is a law of money abundance and implies that you return ten percent of the money you earn to the source of your spiritual substance. Money is a form of energy, and all energy comes from God or the Source of all life. The more we give, the more we will receive in financial wealth.

This concept may be hard for most people to understand, but it is the way to receive more financial wealth and abundance into your life. Some people say that you should give the ten percent back to your church or support a cause that is close to your heart.

I personally believe you should give it to the source of your personal spiritual substance. My spiritual sustenance comes from nature, which to me is God's church. I know people in Alcoholics Anonymous who get their spiritual substance through group support and caring, and they return their ten percent to them.

Search within your personal heart and feel the source of your spiritual sustenance: nature, friends, spiritual community, and family? Start tithing ten percent of your income there. You will see a difference in how fast your abundance flows to you.

Exercise 4

Meditation

What we intellectually understand, we may not always recognize as truth in our heart. To help you know the truth of what supports your spiritual substance, try this meditation exercise.

Close your eyes, and take several deep breaths. Say to yourself, "I am ready to know, see, hear, and be aware of the earthly manifestation of my spiritual support." Then take another deep breath and relax. There is nothing more for you to do except breathe deeply and relax while you wait for the information.

Your mind and body will allow the pictures, words, or feelings to flood you within several minutes. When you are clear and sure of your answer, write it below. Next, send a tithe to this source, and watch for your ten-fold return. When you receive it, also record this answer. To record your tithe and the universe's response to you serves as a reminder that all potential awaits you in this abundant universe. All is possible! You can

read it for yourself on this page!

I gave my tithe to this source in the amount of.....................

The universe returned my ten-fold gift in this form.....................

Angel Quote 5

Call on the angels of abundance and
feel yourself flying high with prosperity

Lesson 5

The Angels of Abundance

Make yourself familiar with the angels, and behold them frequently in

spirit; for without being seen, they are present with you.

- Francis de Sales

Are you starting to reap the rewards of your tithing efforts? It always feels good to give, doesn't it? Giving by itself produces abundant feelings that connect us to the Abundance Angels.

Three primary Angels of Abundance work only with abundance. You can call on these angels anytime to help you bring abundance into your life. Note that they help you create your abundance; they do not do it for you. They can feel your desires and prayers.

The first angel is Anuauel, who holds domination over success, commerce, and financial prosperity. You should ask this angel when you wish for these things in your life.

The second angel is Barakiel, and this one grants good fortune and luck. Call on him when you want to pick Lotto numbers.

The third angel is Sofiel. She is the angel of abundance and great spiritual growth. You call on her when you want spiritual abundance and more growth in your life.

These angels help bring abundance into your life. Never be afraid to ask them to help you. Your angels love to help you. They send you love and blessings.

Exercise 5

Meditation on Angels

After preparing yourself for the meditative state, follow this sequence of steps to meditate with the angel of your choice. With eyes closed, call the Angel by name to you: *Angel _____, I am ready to know, feel, and be aware of your presence.* Then wait. The angel may come to you in one of several ways:

- May Enter your heart chakra, flooding you with their loving presence

- Standing behind you with placing their hand on your shoulders

- Placing their loving hands on your crown chakra, filling you with warmth

- Standing before you, sending healing energy that activates your third eye

- Send swirling loving energy around you and through you

- Approach you with color and sound

- May present themselves in the way that only you receive, like sharing private space between the two of you in love and light.

When you feel present fully with the angel, recognizing the familiar energy, the next step is to make your request. Then be silent and wait for any response.

Record your experience here. Watch for your angelic abundance to manifest, and make note of how this angel works on your behalf.

_____

_____

_____

_____

_____

_____

_____

_____

_____

_____

Angel Quote 6

*Hey, I am your guardian angel and
you haven't written in a while*

Lesson 6

Writing a Letter to Your Guardian Angel

See, I am sending an angel before you, to guard you on the way and bring you to the place I have prepared.

Exodus 23:20

Your personal guardian angel also wants to help bring you abundance. A great way to ask your guardian angel to help you is to write a letter. Yes, just sit down now with the page from Exercise 6.

Then write a letter to your angel asking for what you desire in your life. Do you wish for more wealth? More love? More friends? Write that in the letter.

The secret is that you cannot ask for abundance for some reason of pride. Nor can you ask for things that might hurt another. You can't ask for someone to leave their husband or wife to be with you. You cannot ask to own a Porsche just to drive around in the world and say, "Look at me!" The prideful aspects come from our personal need, not necessarily from our higher good.

Do you remember our discussion on the law of what you reap is what you sow? It applies here. You can ask for money, good health, Porsches, and a better relationship with the one you love for yourself. When you are finished with your letter, sign it.

Once your letter is completed, burn it and send the ashes outside to the angels. Our guardian angels love to help us. Will you receive their help in bringing the abundance that you deserve?

When we stop thinking about our desires for abundance and put them in writing, magic happens. Writing is action that makes our request or desire concrete in the physical world. We can read it, see it, and speak it. We have moved it from our head and made it tangible. Happy letter writing!

Exercise 6

TO MY OWN GUARDIAN ANGEL

Thank You Guardian Angel!

Angel Quote 7

Count your blessings;
see how many more I bring to you
~GOD~

Lesson 7

Living in Gratitude

If you concentrate on finding what is good in every situation, you will

discover that your life will suddenly be filled with gratitude, a feeling that

nurtures the soul.

Rabbi Harold Kushner

Angels tell me that gratitude is the most important attitude to hold if we wish to attract abundance in our lives. Most people tend to focus on the loss they have experienced or the items they do not have. Instead, we need to focus on what we do have and be thankful for these. To attract abundance in our lives, we are to thank God for all the blessings he has given us. Do this every morning.

When we live in gratitude for the things we have, God will bring into our lives even bigger things that we can appreciate and be grateful for. Every day, please count your blessings. Live in gratitude, and then watch your abundance in all areas of your life start to grow.

Exercise 7

Today I am most grateful for . . .

_____

_____

_____

_____

_____

_____

_____

_____

_____

_____

_____

_____

_____

_____

_____

_____

_____

_____

_____

_____

Always look at what you have left. Never look at what you have lost.
Robert H. Schuller

Angel Quote 8

Yes, I ALWAYS hear your prayers.
Why don't you ask me for prosperity more often?

Lesson 8

Your Prayers for Prosperity

Count your blessings. Once you realize how valuable you are and how much you have going for you, the smiles will return, the sun will break out, the music will play, and you will finally be able to move forward to the life that God intended for you with grace, strength, courage, and confidence.

Og Mandino

I know all of you are living with gratitude in your heart. Living like this brightens your heart and feels wonderful. Each morning upon rising, I thank God for three things that I am grateful for in my life. This practice starts my day on a great note.

Today as we discuss *Your Prayers for Prosperity*, imagine these prayers bringing abundance to you. God hears us anytime we pray, so why not say small prayers throughout the day to keep your abundant energy at high levels.

This keeps the association of God and abundance in the forefront of your thoughts at all times. You can make up your own prayers. Mention your gratitude. Keep your prayers simple and say them aloud or hold them privately in your thoughts. All manners of prayers attract the abundance you desire.

Here is an example of one simple prayer: *"God, bring me abundance in all areas of my life. Fill me with a steady supply of money, health, and love. Fill me with spiritual wisdom and growth."* In gratitude, I end each prayer with *"Thank you, God,"* as if my prayers are granted already; because they are.

Do not be afraid to ask for what you truly desire and need. Trust and have faith in knowing you are loved and worthy. If you have trouble creating your own prayer, here is one I use on a daily basis:

"The universe supplies all my needs. All my bills are paid on time. I am debt free and abundant in all areas of my life. Thank you, God."

Then repeat it: "The universe supplies all my needs. All my bills are paid on time. I am debt free and abundant in all areas of my life. Thank you, God."

Happy praying! Enjoy this lesson and remember it always.

Lesson 8

.My Prayers for Prosperity

-----In gratitude!

Angel Quote 9

*A bill is a blessing for things
you have already received.
Think on that for a while.*

Lesson 9

Blessings: Incoming and Outgoing of Money

A prayer of gratitude each day

Keep fears and unworthiness away

Caron Goode, Ed.D.

As you keep your prayers for prosperity in your thoughts each day, there is another step in the abundance mindset to bring into your daily life. In this lesson, I tell you that it is important to bless your money and the bills you pay. When you receive a paycheck or any form of money, hold it for a few seconds. While doing so, silently thank God for sending it to you.

When you pay your bills, hold them to your heart and say, "Thank you God for this blessing also." Know that you are thanking God for the house you live in when you pay your house payment. When you pay any bills, bless them and thank God for them. Bills are blessings for things we have already gotten to enjoy and use. When you start doing this, you will find that soon you have more money coming in than you have going out. I am a witness to the success of this practice. May you be also!

Exercise 9

Meditation: God Speaks to Me, This is How I Listen

When I close my eyes in contemplation, I turn inward. The noise of the outside world washes over me gently and does not distract me. I breathe in a rhythmic, gentle manner so that my body relaxes. I am completely receptive and open. I am relaxed and calm. I am listening, God. I listen with my mind. I listen with my heart. I hear with my whole, intuitive being.

I float in silence. I am silence.

I breathe silence. I listen.

I float in Light. I am Light.

I breathe Light. I feel.

I float in Love. I am Love.

I breathe Love. I know.

I float within God. I am of God.

I breathe God. I Am.

The Way God speaks to me is.....

_____

_____

_____

_____

_____

_____

_____

_____

_____

_____

_____

Angel Quote 10

Dare to ALWAYS dream big.
Nothing is beyond your reach

Lesson 10

Prosperity Dream Board

Build your Own dream instead of

borrowing dreams of others.

Randy Gages

My angels recommend that a visual reminder of your desires will help with prosperity mindfulness. Make yourself a prosperity dream board and place it where you will see it everyday. I have mine on the wall right across from my bed. That way, it is the last thing that I see before I go to sleep. In addition, it is the first thing I look at when I awaken in the morning. Where would you put your prosperity dream board to insure that you focus on it each day, making it visible to the conscious and unconscious mind?

On your prosperity dream board, you place pictures of the abundance you want in your life. Have fun with it. Make it like a scrapbook project. Cut pictures out of magazines that represent your abundant desires: the houses you want to live in, pictures of money or relationship pictures, and perhaps even the perfect car. Do not forget that you are deserving of the luxuries of life also, whether they are vacation, diamonds, or other jewelry.

Most important, put an angel picture on your prosperity dream board to remind you to communicate with your angels daily.

If you want love or a better relationship in your life, put a picture of two people holding hands. If you want to lose weight, put a picture of a thin person on your board. I put such a picture on my board, and I took a picture of myself and put my face in that thin body picture. It is working.

You can put words on your board that inspire you like, "Hey, I'm rich. I'm thin. I'm going to France. I have the most spiritual awakened awareness and connection with my angels."

Our thoughts are like our prayers. The angels don't know any difference between a thought and a prayer. Think about it. When you are praying, the prayers are thoughts. So, if I stand in the mirror in the morning and think, "I look fat;" my angel says, "Hey Carrie thinks she looks fat." You do not want to create that prayer or result in your life.

The more we look at our board and clarify our thoughts, then according to the angels, our prayers bring us these desires. Make your dream board a fun family project and share the desires. A dream board is a good project to share with children in teaching them to focus their mind and stay attuned to their angels. Children have their own dreams and visions.

Lesson 10

Planning My Prosperity Dream Board

Desires

To Include

Thoughts for focus

Thoughts for gratitude

Angel Quote 11

Stones carry special energy so handle them with care.

Holding them, feeling them allow their energy to be

shared

Lesson 11

Stones of Abundance

The best and most beautiful things in the world cannot be seen or even touched.

They must be felt with the heart.

Helen Keller

All stones carry energy and many can draw abundance to us. Today I am giving you a list of some of these stones that bring us abundance. When you wear the particular stones or carry them with you, they will attract the abundance you desire.

Stones that will attract money to you are citrine, pyrite, diamond, and jade. Stones that will attract better health to you are lapis, malachite, and emerald. Stones that attract love to you are rose quartz. Stones that attract your psychic ability will be an amethyst. And the stone to keep away negativity is smoky quartz. Enjoy finding and wearing the stones

that attract the abundance you desire.

Exercise 11

Meditation: Knowing the

Energy of Abundance Stones

Situate your abundance stones in any design in front of you. Be artistic
and follow your intuition when placing the stones. Next, follow this
procedure for each stone and then make notes as you go along. Hold the
stone in your left palm that rests in your right palm. Breathe deeply;
relaxing, and allowing the stone radiance to permeate your feeling and
knowing. Sit with it until you "know the stone." Then write down the
information you received to help you attract your desires using these
stones:

Stones that attract money

Citrine_____

Pyrite_____

Diamond_____

Jade_____

Stones that attract better health

Lapis_____

Malachite _____

Emerald _____

Stones that attracts love

Rose _____

Quartz _____

Stone that attracts psychic ability

Amethyst_____

Stone that keeps away negativity

Smoky Quartz_____

Angel Quote 12

Fragrances for financial wealth and love is a great way
to make even life's rough times feel like everything
is coming up roses.

Lesson 12

Oils of Abundance

Don't limit God's ability to do by your capacity to receive.

Randall D. Worley

Oils of Abundance are so named because they enhance your energy field by their properties and blends. You can use the fragrances that attract abundance in different ways. You can wear oil; put it on your money and in your bathwater; and sprinkle it around your home and office. Do not take any chances on missing any abundance.

To enhance your prosperity radiance, use these fragrances: almond, frankincense, ginger, jasmine, or mint. To attract love, use these fragrances: rose or patchouli. To enhance your psychic ability, use these fragrances: sandalwood and lilac.

You can also buy different oils at your favorite store that will serve your intentions. Some stores may let you blend your own fragrances although most of the blends are premixed for your purposes. Burning incense of the above fragrances also works. This is great fun. What a nice thought: money and love, plus likeability. May your nose experience delight in the delicate scents.

Exercise 12

Experience an Oil of Abundance

Intuitively feel each oil. Do any specific oils strongly attract you?

Pick the top three that intuitively invite you to experience their essence.

Use one abundance oil at a time for three days. Record your experiences

to verify your intuition and to understand more deeply how using these oils

enhance your radiance.

How I felt when I wore the abundance oil was...

I noticed this difference in my energy...

I was attracting...

My angels brought me...

Angel Quote 13

Never be afraid of abundance..
Embrace it with your whole soul.

Lesson 13

Feeling Afraid of Prosperity

When you run from or deny your fear, you leave the Gift unopened.

Lisa Jimenez

One primary reason we block ourselves from abundance is that we feel unworthy. We may harbor feelings that we are undeserving of receiving wealth. Another block might be that we do not want the responsibility of large sums of money.

In our subconscious thoughts, we believe that being abundant is bad due to how we were taught. Think about how some people talk about others with wealth. They say things like, "Those people are filthy rich." Hearing those words makes our subconscious minds associate the two words; and then we believe that if we are rich, we are filthy.

We have heard people say things like, "The rich get richer, and the poor get poorer." All of these words and many more go into our thoughts on a subconscious level and make us feel that it is bad to be abundant.

Really, think about this for a minute. How many times have you heard people say good things about wealthy people? Hey, if you're going to be filthy rich, why would you want to be rich? Think about the movies you have watched. How many of these movies portray these wealthy people to be boring or selfish? There are several ways that you can rid yourself of fears to your abundance.

First, ask your guardian angels to take away any blocks you have that make you fear abundance.

Second, listen to my *Temple of Healing* CD every night. It works on the subconscious mind to take away all the blocks. Listening to the CD opens your subconscious mind to be positive thoughts such as *I am going to be rich.*

The Secret Desserts of Life: http:// www.angelvision29.com

Third, from this day forward, avoid negative thoughts about people and abundance. Look at wealthy people as who you are becoming. Feel joy for them as they are living their birthright and they deserve all that prosperity just as you do.

Remember, prosperity is your birthright!!.

Exercise 13

Clearing Blocks to Abundance

In this exercise, you will write from a stream of consciousness, putting your pen to paper (or fingers to keyboard) and write or type until you feel complete with each phrase. The statements on the next page are closure exercises, because the phrase stimulates all thinking about a topic. Step 1 is to complete the sentence with as many phrases as possible. Step 2 is to turn all negative statements into affirmations. Step 3 is to read or listen to these affirmations daily to reprogram yourself. Here is an example:

Phrase	Written Responses	Affirmations
Money is	Gone	Money is present in my life
	Dirty	Money is clean energy
	Not mine	Money is mine
	Absent from my life	Money is present for me
Rich people are	Snobs	Rich people are friendly
	Unconscious	Rich people are conscious

On the next page is a chart for your personal use. Make as many copies as you need to write, clear, and reaffirm. Have fun!

Your Phrases	Your Written Responses	Your Affirmations

Angel Quote 14

You are worthy of having all that your heart desires,
Be open to receiving it from God

Lesson 14
Feeling Worthy

It's not what a man is worth, but the worthiness of the man.
Joseph P Martino

Today's lesson, Feeling Worthy, focuses on rooting out the cause or block of not feeling worthy. The angels indicate that a major hindrance to bringing all abundance to us is not feeling worthy of receiving it. There could be many reasons for this feeling. Maybe we don't have a great job right now or we are overweight, have low self worth, or are moving through an emotional time in our lives. Sometimes we do not even feel worthy of great health because someone we loved died and we could not help them.

The angels relate to all of us that you are worthy of all the abundance in this world. God offers all the abundance to you. The angels provide this great affirmation for you to use to get out of the deepest trenches of unworthy feelings. Say this aloud or in your thoughts whenever you feel unworthy:

"I am worthy of receiving the entire abundance that God

and the universe offer me because it is my birthright."

When you say it, feel it in your very soul. "I am worthy of receiving the entire abundance that God and the universe offer me because it's my birthright." Now can you feel it? "I am worthy of receiving the entire abundance that God and the universe offer because it is my birthright."

Now, say it, feel it, and think it every day; and the unworthiness issues that you have will leave you.

Exercise 14

My Daily Abundance Affirmation

I am worthy of receiving

the entire abundance that God

and the universe offers me

because it is my birthright.

Angel Quote 15

Performing random acts of kindness makes

the universe sing with happiness.

Lesson 15

Random Acts of Kindness

We wildly underestimate the power of the

tiniest personal touch of kindness.

Author Unknown

Today the angels address how performing random acts of kindness will bring abundance to you. Random acts of kindness for others return to us tenfold, according to the law of what we sow, we shall reap. An act of kindness is a gift of your heart, not necessarily of money. Just give from your heart. That's the important part. I often buy roses and give them out one at a time.

That random act of kindness brought me the most beautiful roses in my yard the year after my daughter, Jennifer, died. I did not feel like tending my yard or the garden that year because I was grieving. Nevertheless, that year I had the most beautiful roses ever. My angels told me that even though I was grieving, I took the time to give out roses randomly to others; and then my roses bloomed for me.

Remember that the energy we send out from our hearts through a random act of kindness spreads love everywhere. It returns to us by bringing us all kinds of random abundance. Like people paying for our dinner, giving us flowers from their garden, or an extra hug from our spouse or our child. Start with random acts of kindness daily and watch how the universe brings it back to you tenfold. This is one of my favorite abundance acts.

Exercise 15

Random Acts of Kindness Weekly Diary

Use the Chart on the next page to fill in your "Daily" Acts of Kindness and what the Universe has given you in exchange for your gifts.

Day	My Act of Kindness	The Universe Returned ...
1		
2		
3		
4		
5		
6		
7		

Angel Quote 16

Love yourself first.

Then you will attract the one you desire.

Lesson 16

Attracting Abundance in Love

All love is Divine. Let it never be said that physical or romantic love is less than God's Love, for ideas cannot be apart from their source.

Alan Cohen

Today, the special abundance lesson is Attracting Abundance in Love. This lesson is about attracting an abundance of love to you. So many people search for that special love relationship more than any other kind of abundance.

One step that you can take to attract your special mate is to write down eleven special qualities you truly desire in a partner. The number eleven has a spiritual vibration that connects us to the angel realm, and eleven qualities of attraction can vibrate to the angelic frequency. That is why we should write down just eleven qualities that portray the partner we intend to attract to ourselves.

After you have written down the eleven qualities, review it every day; and pray, "My angels and the universe are now bringing my perfect love mate and me together." Once again, "My angels and the universe are now bringing my perfect love mate and me together. Thank you."

I have had many clients attract the love of their life to them this way. I would also wear the fragrances that attract love to you like rose and patchouli fragrances.

Exercise 16

Eleven Qualities I Desire In My Partner

Use the Chart on the next page to fill in your Eleven Qualities that you "Desire" in your Partner

Number   Quality

1

2

3

4

5

6

7

8

9

10

11

Angel Quote 17

Keep your chakras balanced, and
feel your life in balance at the same time

Lesson 17

Chakra Balancing

Becoming and being are the yin and yang of our lives. One inner one outer.

Today, we value becoming to the exclusion of being; we applaud human

becomings.

The secret is balance.

Author Unknown

Today's lesson is Chakra Balancing. The chakras are energy centers that connect to the nerve centers along our brain and central nervous system. They vibrate at different frequency levels and circulate energy, connecting our physical bodies and the world of energy.

For this lesson on abundance, the angels suggest that you must keep all of your chakras in balance if you want to keep the flow of abundance coming to you. Keep blocks from forming in your chakras. For example, a block in your heart chakra keeps you from attracting love. Blocks in other chakras also keep you from financial abundance as well as from good physical or emotional health. To attract abundance to you and all areas of your life, you must keep your chakras in a balance and free from blocks. The next exercise can help you with this.

Exercise 17

Meditation - Chakra Balance

I close my eyes and breathe the energy of balance and abundance. As I relax my body, the color of abundance swirls at my feet. I prepare to cleanse and balance my chakras. My intention is to breathe the swirl of cleansing Light up through the soles of my feet.

Each breath that I take pulls the abundant Light up through my ankles, rising up my legs to my knees. The light rises upward, entering my thighs and moving to my hips, touching the base of my spine.

Each breath that I take pulls the abundant, cleansing color up though my body—crawling up my spine gently calming every nerve fiber—washing each organ and bone as it moves up.

Each breath I take moves the abundant, clarifying Light straight up

through my throat and head, showering my body, aura, and chakra

system.

Angel Quote 18

Hug a tree to make
your heart a happy one.

Lesson 18

Attracting Money with Trees

Be a gentle friend to trees and they will give you back beauty,

cool and fragrant shade, and many birds, singing.[1]

Anonymous

Today's lesson is called Attracting Money with Trees. This one sounds strange, doesn't it? The Native American Indians feel, as I do, that trees heal; and they can bring abundance to the world and to us.

Have you ever hugged a tree and felt its beautiful energy? It feels great to restore my energy by hugging a tree, which I do often. Here is a list of what specific trees will bring you. Planting these trees, sitting by these trees, or carrying a piece of them will bring you the type of

---

[1] http://www.inspirational-quotations.com/nature-quotes.html

...abundance that they attract.

- **Acorns from the Oak trees** will grant financial success and wishes of prosperity to you.

- **Cedar trees** keep you on your spiritual path and help you become more psychic.

- **Fruit trees** of any kind bring abundance in all areas of our lives.

- **Walnut trees** grant us the ability to manifest money through prayers. Remember to pray to your angels in this regard.

- **Pine fosters** within us the courage to seek our fortune. It also heals us physically and emotionally. I carry a pinecone in my pocket often.

Exercise 18

Knowing Tree Energy

In order to know the fullest gift of a tree's nature, it is best to attune to the flow of sap in the tree. To begin, choose one of three different physical postures to be comfortable with the tree

1. Sit at the base of the tree with your erect spine resting on the tree trunk.

2. Standing with an erect spine against the tree, leaning inward against the tree trunk to support yourself.

3. Hugging the tree, arms stretched around the tree while resting the front of your body against the trunk comfortably.

Notice that each of these positions allows your chakras to align with the tree. Closing your eyes and breathing deeply, melt into the tree. Project your consciousness into the tree's center, connecting with the flow of the sap which is the lifeblood of the tree.

Continue breathing until you feel completely immersed in the experience, moving with the sap. Then, ask the tree about its relationship to you and your abundance. Actually, you can be aware of all energy through your knowing.

Blessed be your abundance.

Angel Quote 19

Live in the now as it is
a gift called the present

Lesson 19

Live in the Now & Stop the Worry Habit

Live in the present moment and find your interest

and happiness in the things of today.

Emmett Fox

The key of today's abundance lesson is in the title itself, Live in the Now and Stop the Worry Habit. The angels said that if you wish to attract abundance to you in all areas of your life, then start living in the now. How do you do this? There are different ways:

- Not letting your mind wander to the past

- Focusing on your task at hand

- Not projecting yourself into the future

- Trusting that what happens is for your learning or for your good.

Trust that God and the universe will take care of everything and know that He will grant your abundance. When we live in the past or future, we always live in stress. Our thoughts become filled with the "What if" and "I should have" or "I need to."

When we live in the now, we are living in faith that God and the universe will take care of everything. Keeping these thoughts in mind will bring our abundance to us in all areas of our lives.

My angel told me when I was young to watch the birds. He told me that even before the birds look for food, they start to sing a song of thanks. They sing because they are happy knowing that God will provide them with everything, all they need.

Let us rise each morning and sing a song of thanks knowing that God is taking care of us and bringing all of us our abundance. Use the letter in the word NOW to bring abundance to you. N-O-W, Notice Only Wonderful abundant things in your life, and that is what you should attract.

Exercise 19

Abundance Affirmation

Notice

Only

Wonderful

Abundance

Angel Quote 20

It's a great thing to be nice to mother nature
and all of her beautiful animals...
we can not survive without them

Lesson 20

Taking Care of Nature

Rest is not idleness, and to lie sometimes on the grass under trees

on a summer's day, listening to the murmur of the water,

or watching the clouds float across the sky is by no means a waste of time.

J. Lubbuck

Today's lesson, Taking Care of Nature, starts with a song in your heart and an ear attuned to both the angels and birds. During my morning prayers, the angels said that we should all take care of Mother Nature if we wish to attract the true abundance in our lives.

Mother Nature is a living, breathing being and provides so much for us. She feeds us, shelters us, and brings us much of our abundance. We need to give back to her. The more we give back to Mother Nature, my angels told me, the more we will receive abundance in all areas of our own life.

In what ways can we give back to Mother Nature on a regular basis? Plant trees, feed the animals, clean up the garbage, and recycle. Blessings come from our angels when we do these things to heal and protect our earth. For all of you who are doing these tasks, the angels say thank you so much.

Mother Nature blesses you through the animals that come your way. Every one of them brings us a spiritual gift when they visit us. Author, Ted Andrews wrote a book called *Animal Speaks*, which describes a gift each animal brings to us. For example, when you see a hawk, it means you are protected and you will receive spiritual abundance. Do the most we can for Mother Nature. She will appreciate it and return the abundance to us.

Exercise 20

Let Nature Touch Your Heart

It is a unique and dynamic experience to walk **with** nature as opposed to taking a walk *in* nature. When attuned to nature, energetically and viscerally, you walk through a wonderland of fauna, elements, and flora that you may not have noticed before. This is how to accomplish the special connection to nature. Find a way to relax completely before walking so that your mind is silent and your breath is open and deep.

On this walk, follow your body. Your body leads the way as if moving you along your private escalator. Let your eyes soften, as if staring through the trees instead of at the leaves and as if peering through space instead of focusing on a bird. Allow your eyes to gaze across landscapes and notice what creature is in your field of awareness. Take this walk three times and each time record your observations of nature – most especially, your inner experience of nature.

_____

_____

_____

_____

_____

_____

_____

_____

_____

_____

Angel Quote 21

Visualize your heart's desires
and feel them manifesting

Lesson 21

Visualizing the Abundance You Desire.

The real voyage of discovery is not in seeking new lands

but in seeing with new eyes.

Marcel Proust

Today's lesson, Visualizing the Abundance You Desire, focuses on how to take the time to visualize and feel the abundance you desire. Close your eyes and envision the car of your dreams. See clearly the color, open the door, sit inside, and smell the new interior. How does it feel to drive the car of your dreams?

Next, see in your mind's eye the house in which you truly want to live. Walk inside and tour the spaces, seeing the colors and textures that make it your dream home.

What we visualize, we bring closer to us. Whatever abundance you are wishing to attract in your life, put yourself in relaxed state and feel the fullest joy of your wealth. Imagine, feel, and imbibe in your wealth.

Write a movie script of what your perfect day would be like and be as descriptive as possible: What job do you have? What kind of house do you live in? What kind of relationships do you have? Write down what your perfect day would be like. Then, look at it often and visualize that day. Read the entire script before going to bed and as you awaken in the morning. By doing this, you will bring that day of perfect abundance to you in your thoughts and carry it with you. Remember, thoughts are like prayers that angels want to grant for us. The more you do this, the more the angels will work at bringing you that perfect abundant day.

Exercise 21

My Perfect Day of Abundance

_____

_____

_____

_____

_____

_____

_____

_____

_____

_____

_____

_____

_____

_____

_____

_____

_____

_____

_____

_____

_____

_____

_____

_____

_____

_____

_____

_____

_____

_____

_____

_____

_____

_____

Angel Quote

Conclusion

Spread seeds of love & light everywhere you go;
and watch the seeds of abundance bear fruit
in all areas of your life

Happy Endings

The secret to a rich life is to have more beginnings than endings.

David Weinbaum

Now, you are on your way to a more abundant life. Use and enjoy the lessons that the angels and I have given you to attract the abundant birthright that God says is yours. The angels send their blessings, and they stand ready to help you attract the abundance in all areas of your life.

Please review these lessons as often as possible as they are the key to your life-long success and abundance. May you always walk in peace my special friend! May you always walk in light and love. May you have all the abundance in your life that you so deserve and desire.

Namaste

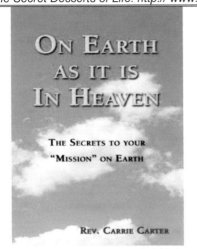

<u>Your Owner's Manual to Your Soul</u>

<u>YES, we can Communicate with Love Ones in the Spirit Realm.</u>

Have you ever wondered why you were put on this earth? Have you ever wondered if there was a rhyme or reason or a "mission" that you are here to fulfill? You will discover a sense of purpose in between the covers of this book. Reverend Carrie is a remarkable woman whose life has revolved around Angels and the Spirit Guide world since she was brought to this Earth Plain to serve her mission. She opens the door for you to the Spirit World within our "Touch" Everyday.

Book Cost: $16.00 + S&H

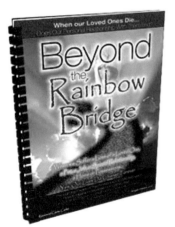

Beyond the Rainbow Bridge:

If you have ever asked yourself these questions:
If I could hug my Loved One, one last time and tell them something special what would it be?
What really goes on during the process we call death?
What can I do after a loved one dies to help THEIR soul process?
How do I know that my Loved One in heaven hears me talking to them?
Do my Loved Ones on the other side know HOW MUCH I DO LOVE THEM?
How do I work through the terrible losses that life sends my way?
How do I start over after I have lost my home, relationship, pet, or job?

This Personal Guide Book is for you to use to understand and get the answers to many of your questions. This is a "Powerful" tool in overcoming the Road Blocks that prevent you from getting through your "Grief" and experiencing the exciting, new journeys that awaits you here on earth before you cross the "Beyond the Rainbow Bridge"

Book Cost: Call Office or Visit Our Website

The Care & Nurturing of Crystal & Indigo Children

This CD was channeled by Reverend Carrie's Angels and is very powerful and positive. The soft background music is a great meditation for all ages. It is especially powerful for our children. It gives positive affirmations like: "You are loved", "You will always be happy", "You will be free of any kind of addictions", "You will be free of all negative input from the world" and "You will find your success without hurting anyone". Reverend Carrie says" My Angels have told me if our children listen to this CD as much as possible, especially when sleeping, they will grow up more in balance with themselves and the world around them. We owe it to our children to give them all this love & positive input."

CD Cost: $18.00 + S&H

Journey to the Temple of Healing

This VERY POWERFUL meditation CD will take you to the Angel's Temple of Healing. You use this CD to heal yourself physically, mentally, emotionally, & spiritually.

Your Angels will also remove from you ALL the negative thoughts and inputs you have had in your life and replace them with positive thought forms. We have all had so much negative input in our lives.

The more you listen to this CD the more that the negative energy in your life will leave you. It will ONLY make you open to positive thoughts coming into your awareness. I feel so very blessed that the Angels have channeled this CD through me.

CD Cost: $18.00 + S&H

Manifesting Your Perfect Body

Within each and every one of us resides our "Perfect Body" just waiting to be sculpted with the hammer, chisels, and granite of our mind. In this CD Reverend Carrie guides you through a positive upbeat meditation, which takes you down the path of health and happiness.

With her words you not only visualize but you "Feel" your body becoming healthier and healthier with each passing minute. You should use this CD as a "Support System" to your own daily Weight Management Program.

CD Cost: $18.00 + S&H

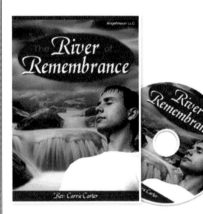

The River of Remembrance

Can you imagine, listening to sweet angelic music as you drift off into meditation where you are greeted by your Guardian Angel. They extend their hand to you and as you grasp it you are taken to the special place in the Universe... **The River of Remembrance**.

As you arrive at this special destination you are in awe of the beauty and serenity that surrounds you. As you become aware of your environment, your Guardian Angel leads you to a magnificent waterfall where your Loved Ones on the other side are waiting to greet you.

With this CD you are able to visit with your loved ones on the other side time after time to feel all the love and caring they still have for you

CD Cost: $18.00 + S&H

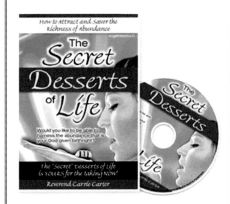

The Secret Desserts of Life

Are you Prosperous in all areas of your life? Are you living the life you always imagined…or have you given up on your dream? Do you wonder why some people have all the luxuries in life, and others don't? If you need to know the answers to these questions, and more this is the CD for you!

The Angel's have blessed Reverend Carrie with their secrets of how to bring abundance to all areas of you life.

These are Hands-On Lessons that will put YOUR Abundance and Prosperity into "High Gear" Listen Over and Over as Reverend Carrie give you some common sense Approaches to use in your Everyday Life

CD Cost: $18.00 + S&H

Ask The Angel Lady

The "Angel Lady" Asks the Angels your most thought provoking questions, in a Live

A 90 Minute Tele-Seminar.

Reverend Carrie will also share with you the answers to over 19 questions that the Angels guarantee will bring you more Peace, Prosperity, Abundance, and Happiness in Your Life. Such As:
   What is my Life's Purpose
   Do we reincarnate over and Over
   Do my pets go to Heaven
   How do I know my Angel's Names

Listen, Enjoy, and Learn…

CD Cost: $28.00 + S&H

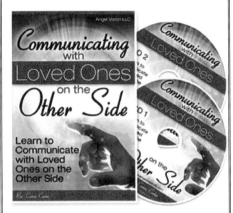

Communicating with Loved Ones on the Other Side

Read – Understand – Live. Have you ever felt like there was something missing in your life? Have you ever wondered why you were put on this earth? Have you ever wondered if there was a rhyme or reason or a "mission" that you are here to fulfill? After listening to this almost 3 hour CD set, you will discover a sense of purpose and most of all understanding

Explore & Discover the Reasons:
Why we all pick our parents. Sometimes we pick them for them to teach us, and sometimes for us to teach them.
How loved Ones communicate with you from the Spirit Realm.
Why & How our souls leaves our body? Why there are Multi-Levels of Heaven. Plus Much More!

CD Cost: $28.00 + S&H

Developing the Goddess Within

In this Awaken the Goddess Within Mini-Course you will discover: What is a Psychic?
What is channeling.
What is Mediumship?
What is an Earth Angel?
The Main lesson we come to Earth to Learn.
What is Psychic Protection?

PS: this CD set is not only for the "Goddess" but it is also for those guys Aspiring to be a "God" in this lifetime as well. This is almost 3 Hours packed with information that will free your soul

CD Cost: $28.00 + S&H

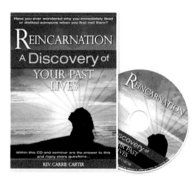

Reincarnation: A Discovery of Your Past Lives

Have you ever questioned past lives?
Would you like to discover what a Soul Mate is and how do you attract one?

Did you realize there are specific reasons that you might fall in love at "First Sight" or dislike someone for no reason at all?

Plus with the guided meditation you will find out about mirror gazing and WHO YOU were in at least one past life time.

You might even uncover someone you know now with whom you shared a past life time.

Plus listening to this CD every second is plain fun, exciting and laughter filled and guaranteed to put a "Smile" on your Face and Uplift your Heart!

CD Cost: $28.00 + S&H

Do you remember as a child that little "Angel Friend" that you spent hours with playing and talking and in times of confusion would tell you what "Right" was and what not to do…

Remember as a child how uplifting and encouraging your little "Angel Friend' was for you when you were feeling sad, unsure, or lost as to what to do.

Remember after school you used to excitedly run home and, bound up those stairs to your room or that "Secret" space no one discovered and how happy you were to play with and talk to your "Angel Friend" all evening long.

Remember how sad you were the day that your parents or friends told you that your special "Angel Friend" didn't exist and "Big" Boys and Girls don't believe in those silly things…"

Have you ever wondered why you always feel like there is just a "Small" part of you missing or longing to be rediscovered… This feeling that you have lost something special but haven't been able to put your finger on the missing parts.

We have reawakened your Angel Friend and have given you a chance to reclaim what you have lost…

We would like to introduce you to "My Angel Coach" This is an animated Reverend Carrie Carter and her Mountain Lion Hercules who will visit your computer screen everyday, every hour or even every few minutes, depending how you set your control panel, to bring you uplifting affirmations and advice that you can put into practice right now.

For a Free 30 day trial join us today and discover how quickly your "Angel Coach" can make a BIG difference in your life… to register go to:

www.AngelLadyCoach.com

SALES ORDER

Angel Vision LLC
12272 Fenton Rd. Suite #3
Fenton, Michigan 48430 USA

Date:

	Mailing Address	Shipping Address
	Names:_____ Address:_____ City:_____ State:_____ Phone:_____	Names:_____ Address:_____ City:_____ State:_____ Phone:_____

Credit Card	Card Number	Expiration Date	CVS Number			

Qty	Item #	Description	Unit Price	Discount	Line Total
			Total Discount		
				Subtotal	
				Sales Tax	
				Total	